W9-AGD-855

Animals of the Night

CROCODILES AND ALLIGATORS AFTER DARK

Ruth O'Shaughnessy

Enslow Publishing
101 W. 23rd Street
Suite 240
New York, NY 10011
USA

enslow.com

Words to Know

carnivore—An animal that eats meat.

crocodilian—A member of the reptile group that crocodiles and alligators belong to.

endangered—In danger of dying out.

marsh—Swampy, wet land.

nocturnal—Active at night.

predator—An animal that hunts other animals for food.

prey—An animal hunted by another animal for food.

reptile—An animal that has a backbone and lungs and is usually covered with scales. Also, its body temperature adjusts to the area it is in.

species—A type of animal.

Contents

Nightfall

Night falls on the Serengeti in Africa. A wildebeest goes to the river for a cool drink. The river is calm and silent. The wildebeest has no idea a hungry crocodile is quietly swimming toward it.

Moments later, the crocodile grabs the wildebeest in its jaws. The wildebeest is pulled into the water. It fights for its life, but it is no match for the crocodile. The crocodile quickly drags the wildebeest beneath the water, and the wildebeest soon drowns. The crocodile will eat until it is full. It will not be hungry for days.

Fun Fact!

Crocodiles can go a long time without eating. Large crocodiles can survive as long as two years without feeding! They live on the fat stored in their tails.

A Nile crocodile lies by the Mara River in Kenya in Africa.

Ancient Crocodilians

Crocodiles and alligators belong to a group of reptiles called crocodilians. Some species, or types, of crocodilians lived more than 200 million years ago. They were around when huge dinosaurs roamed Earth.

Back then, a few crocodilians were as big as dinosaurs. Among the largest of these was *Sarcosuchus* (SAR-co-suk-us) *imperator* or "flesh crocodile emperor." This crocodilian was 40 feet (12 meters) long. It weighed 10 tons (9 metric tons)— about as much as five cars! *Sarcosuchus* is also called "SuperCroc." Like the dinosaurs, the SuperCroc died out.

Fun Fact!

Crocodilians are more closely related to birds than to lizards.

A worker at a zoo places the skull of a Nile crocodile inside the jaws of a SuperCroc skull to show how huge SuperCroc was.

Giant Reptiles

There are fourteen different species of crocodiles and two species of alligator. Most adult crocodiles are about 8 to 12 feet (2 ½ to 4 meters) long. Some Australian saltwater crocodiles have grown to more than 20 feet (6 meters), about as long as a bus. The American alligator grows to about 8 to 10 feet (2 ½ to 3 meters) but can be as long as 19 feet (6 meters).

Like all reptiles, alligator and crocodile body temperatures change to match the area the reptile is in. On cool mornings, alligators and crocodiles often rest in the sun. This heats them up. When it gets too hot, they cool off in the water.

An alligator soaks up the sunshine to warm itself.

Physical Traits

Crocodiles and alligators share many features because they are related to each other. They have rough, scaly skin with bony plates on their backs. They both have sharp, pointed teeth that are constantly replaced when they fall out.

Both crocodiles and alligators are also good swimmers. Their long, slim bodies move well in the water. They use their strong tails as paddles to push them along. Sometimes they will lash out at an enemy with their tails.

Fun Fact!

A crocodile's bite is stronger than any other animal's in the world.

A crocodile never runs out of teeth.

Alligator or Crocodile?

Although there are many similarities between crocodiles and alligators, there are some differences too. A crocodile has a narrow V-shaped head. This helps them hunt fish, birds, and other animals. An alligator's head is wider and rounder. It is shaped like a U. An alligator's snout is designed to be strong enough to crack open the shells of turtles and other animals that they eat.

The fourth tooth on a crocodile's lower jaw shows when its mouth is closed. This tooth is hidden when an alligator's mouth is closed. Also, crocodiles are considered to be more aggressive than alligators. They are more likely to attack.

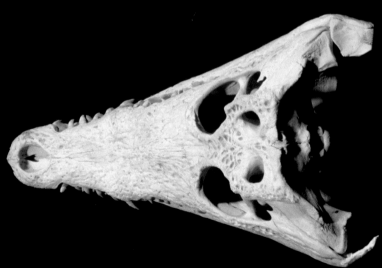

An alligator's head
(top) is broader than
a crocodile's head
(bottom).

Nocturnal Hunters

Crocodiles and alligators are mostly **nocturnal**, which means they are more active at night. They see well in the dark because like cats' eyes, the eyes of crocodiles and alligators have pupils that change shape. The pupils narrow into slits during the day and widen at night to let more light in. Crocodiles and alligators can spot **prey** that might not see them. They can also smell and hear nearby animals after dark. Crocodile and alligator ears are small openings located behind the eyes. These reptiles do not need daylight to find a meal.

An American alligator
swims at night, looking
for prey.

Carnivores

Crocodiles and alligators are **carnivores**, which means they eat meat. Smaller alligators and crocodiles usually eat fish, turtles, birds, and frogs. Bigger ones eat monkeys, oxen, pigs, deer, antelope, and other large animals.

Crocodiles and alligators are ambush **predators**, which means they sneak up on their prey and then attack. It is hard to see these reptiles in the water. Sometimes they look like floating logs. Other times, only their eyes and nostrils show.

Fun Fact!

The American alligator can stay underwater for up to two hours.

A crocodile feasts on a fish.

Crocodiles and alligators grab their prey with their powerful jaws. They usually drag the animal into the water. Crocodiles and alligators do not chew their food. They swallow small prey whole. These meals go down in one gulp.

Eating larger prey takes more work. Crocodiles and alligators twist and pull off parts of their prey's body. This move is sometimes called a death roll. The pieces of meat are swallowed in one gulp as well. Crocodiles and alligators throw back their heads while swallowing. This makes the food fall down their throats.

An American alligator appears in the murky water. This would be the last thing its prey would see before being pulled into the water.

Warm Habitats

Crocodiles and alligators live in warm weather climates. Crocodiles live in the hottest parts of Africa, Australia, Southeast Asia, and North and South America.

Some species of crocodiles live in salty waters near the ocean. Other types of crocodiles live in freshwater. These are found in swamps, lakes, and other freshwater spots. And some crocodiles live in both saltwater and freshwater.

Fun Fact!

Ancient crocodile mummies have been found in Egypt.

Two Nile crocodiles bask in the sun with their mouths open in Africa. This is called gaping.

American alligators mostly live in the southeastern United States. They are in Alabama, Arkansas, North and South Carolina, Florida, Georgia, Louisiana, Mississippi, Oklahoma, and Texas. They live in freshwater habitats such as swamps, marshes, ponds, lakes, canals, and some rivers.

Fun Fact!

Crocodiles and alligators can swim up to 20 miles (32 kilometers) per hour!

This American alligator lives in the Everglades, an area of wetlands in Florida.

Survival in the Wild

Adult crocodiles and alligators are large, strong, and fierce. They do not have many predators to fear. However, large snakes in Asia have attacked crocodiles. In Florida, big snakes have attacked alligators as well.

Occasionally, crocodiles and alligators are killed while they are hunting. Crocodiles sometimes attack the babies of big animals such as elephants. If the mothers of these animals are nearby, they defend their babies. A mother elephant can kill a crocodile threatening her baby.

Very young crocodiles and alligators cannot defend themselves. Snakes, raccoons, turtles, owls, and other animals eat them. Large crocodiles and alligators sometimes eat smaller ones as well.

Two baby American alligators hang on to their mother. She protects them from danger.

Family Life

Although crocodiles and alligators are related, they cannot have babies with each other. They mate with members of their own species. After mating, the female builds a nest.

Some female crocodiles dig a hole in the sand where they lay their eggs. Then they cover the eggs with sand, making little hills, or mounds. Others build mound nests of soil, leaves, and twigs.

Female alligators build mound nests too. They lay their eggs in the center of the mound. Then they cover the eggs and stay close by to guard the nest.

Female crocodiles and alligators stay with their babies for about two years. They carry them to the water in their mouths. They also try to protect them from predators.

Fun Fact!

Crocodiles and alligators keep growing all their lives.

A baby Nile crocodile hatches from an egg. It will depend on its mother until it is big enough to survive on its own.

Relationship with People

The only predator that alligators and crocodiles are threatened by is people. People used to hunt all different kinds of crocodiles and alligators for their skins to make and sell handbags, belts, and shoes. Many crocodiles and alligators died off when swamps and wetlands were drained to build farms and towns. Boats scared them away from their nesting areas, and each year many eggs were destroyed or could not hatch.

Over time, some species of crocodiles and alligators became **endangered**, or in danger of dying out. Some countries passed laws to protect these animals. Before long, the numbers of crocodiles and alligators began to rise. Today, people still make and sell items made from alligator and crocodile skins, but there are rules in place to make sure only nonendangered species are used.

Reptile expert Joe Wasilewski releases a baby crocodile into a canal in Florida. He works to save crocodiles and other reptiles.

Stay Safe Around Alligators and Crocodiles

There are some places, such as areas of Florida or Central America, where people live near alligators and crocodiles. These animals have a natural fear of humans and do not usually look for people to attack. It is best to keep it that way since they may attack if people get too close. If you live or visit places where there are crocodiles or alligators, follow these safety tips:

 Stay away from crocodiles or alligators.

 Do not feed these reptiles. It makes them lose their fear of humans.

 Never tease these animals or throw anything at them.

 Do not swim where you know there are crocodiles or alligators.

 Crocodiles and alligators can never be pets. They are wild animals.

 If you see an alligator or crocodile in an area where there's a lot of people, tell an adult so he or she can call your state's wildlife agency.

Learn More

Books

Furstinger, Nancy. *Alligators*. Edina, Minn.: Core Library, 2014.

Gagne, Tammy. *Crocodile*. Edina, Minn.: Core Library, 2013.

Gray, Susan H. *American Alligator*. North Mankato, Minn.: Cherry Lake Publishing, 2013.

Schafer, Susan. *Saltwater Crocodiles*. New York: Cavendish Square Publishing, 2014.

Web Sites

kids.sandiegozoo.org/animals/reptiles/american-alligator

Learn fun facts about the American alligator, such as where it lives, what it eats, and where the word *alligator* comes from.

animals.sandiegozoo.org/animals/crocodilian

Read all about the crocodilians, the reptile group alligators and crocodiles belong to.

kids.nationalgeographic.com/content/kids/en_US/animals/nile-crocodile/

Discover how large the Nile crocodile really is and watch videos starring this awesome reptile.

Index

Published in 2016 by Enslow Publishing, LLC.
101 W. 23rd Street, Suite 240, New York, NY 10011

Library of Congress Cataloging-in-Publication Data
O'Shaughnessy, Ruth, author.
  Crocodiles and alligators after dark / Ruth O'Shaughnessy.
    pages cm. — (Animals of the night)
  Summary: "Discusses crocodiles and alligators, their behavior, and
    environment"—Provided by publisher.
  Audience: Ages 8+
  Audience: Grades 4 to 6.
  Includes bibliographical references and index.
  ISBN 978-0-7660-6756-1 (library binding)
  ISBN 978-0-7660-6754-7 (pbk.)
  ISBN 978-0-7660-6755-4 (6-pack)
  1. Crocodiles—Juvenile literature. 2. Alligators—Juvenile literature.
    3. Nocturnal animals—Juvenile literature. 4. Animal behavior—
    Juvenile literature. I. Title.
  QL666.C925O83 2016
  597.98—dc23
                        2015009967

Printed in the United States of America

Portions of this book originally appeared in the book *Alligators and
Crocodiles: Hunters of the Night*.

Photo Credits: Alexander Rieber/EyeEm/Getty Images (crocodile),
p. 1; © AP Images, p. 7; David Tipling/Photographer's Choice/Getty
Images, p. 5; Eye Ubiquitous/Universal Images Group/Getty Images,
p. 9; James H. Robinson/Science Source/Getty Images, p. 25; James
P. Blair/National Geographic/Getty Images, p. 15; Jim Abernathy/
National Geographic/Getty Images, p. 19; Joe McDonald/Visuals
Unlimited/Getty Images, p. 13; Joe Readle/Getty Images, p. 29; John
Lund/Stone/Getty Images, pp. 3, 11; kimberrywood/Digital Vision
Vectors/Getty Images (green moon dingbats); Martin Harvey/
Gallo Images/Getty Images, pp. 17, 27; narvikk/E+/Getty Images
(starry background); Nigel Pavitt/AWL Images/Getty Images, p.
21; samxmeg/E+/Getty Images (moon folios and series logo);
Thinkstock/Stockbite/Getty Images, p. 23.

Cover Credits: Alexander Rieber/EyeEm/Getty Images (crocodile);
narvikk/E+/Getty Images (starry backgroud) kimberrywood/Digital
Vision Vectors/Getty Images (green moon dingbat); samxmeg/E+/
Getty Images (moon).